CW01266018

£5.00

German Swearing:
Top German Insults
and How to Use Them
(A Quick and Dirty Guide)

By Dirk Purrucker

Table of Contents

The way Germans speak, well…this is a language that sounds *pissed off*, so they must love swearing, right?

Surprisingly, Germans don't whole-heartedly embrace swearing. While it is not necessarily seen as a negative thing in Germany, and it is rather common for people of all ages, genders and classes to let 'er rip, there are some rather stringent, unspoken rules about cussing. While it is generally accepted to use mild swear words as part of your daily vernacular, harsh swear words or politically incorrect swear words (for instance, those that discriminate one's race or physical and mental disabilities) are not acceptable in your local grocery store, and are generally only used by young people or the lower class.

Old people do swear, but only with the common or mild swear words. Those might include *scheisse* (shit), *mist* (damn), *verdammt* (damn), *idiot* (idiot).

People at work only swear very mildly and mainly do so among colleagues, not with higher-ups. It is negative to swear while interacting with clients or customers.

Swearing at school is a definite cause for punishment. Between friends it is common enough to swear, and mild swearing is also not seen as a very negative aspect in a family setting.

Among the younger set since the 1990s, a lot of politically incorrect swear words have evolved, such as *behindert,* which means "retarded." Cusses like these are now very common with youths; however, older people would consider them highly unsuitable. Politically incorrect swear words mainly apply to disabilities, gender or sexual orientation.

In the lower classes swearing was always very common, but in the higher classes it was viewed as a very bad habit. This changed during the second half of the twentieth century. In certain settings it is still totally inappropriate (as in America); people belonging to a royal family, politicians or professors, for instance, would not use swear words and even avoid the very mild ones. Generally speaking, it has become more common for the higher and the middle class to use swear words.

This guide brings you the most common German swear words, running the gamut from mild to harsh, with their English equivalent. You will see what they mean, how they originated and who tends to use them, as well as examples of use in both German and English.

Insults for the Ladies

When women get into a fight, a real screaming match of an argument, watch the hell out. Usually the gloves come off — if there were any gloves to begin with. Whether the women in question are emotional basket-cases or cold snakes, when they have something derogatory to say to one another they will usually use any number of these following words/phrases, usually in some cutting combination. If you need to put a woman in her place while you're in Germany, use these, but don't be surprised if she flings them right back at you.

1. Slut: *Schlampe*

All throughout history, if you wanted to destroy a woman's reputation, you attacked her by calling her lustful and telling everyone that she likes to have sex a lot, usually indiscriminately. While that kind of behavior is much more acceptable in today's modern society (even celebrated, depending on who you ask!), calling a woman a slut — behind her back, to her face, but always in front of others — is still the easiest way to turn public opinion against her. If some German tart comes along and tries to snag your lover from under your nose, she's definitely a "Schlampe" of the first water!

Explanation: *Schlampe* has been used in the past and is still used by some older people as a word to describe a dirty woman, someone who does not take care of herself and is untidy. Nowadays it is mainly used to describe women that have sex with various different men or wear suggestive clothes. *Schlampe* is seen as a very vulgar word and is mainly used by younger people.

Example: Look at what that girl is wearing, what a slut.

Guck mal, was das Mädchen anhat was eine Schlampe.

3

2. Whore: *Nutte*

If you want to connote the idea that the woman in question likes to have sex for money (is that better or worse? It's up to you to decide!), try "nutte" instead. Let your pal imagine that the woman you're talking about goes and stands on the street corner looking like shorter, wider version of Julia Roberts in Pretty Woman. That'll teach her!

Explanation: Nutte originated in Berlin in the late 19th century as a word for a prostitute. It had been used prior to describe the female genitals. Nutte is seen as a very vulgar word and mainly used by younger people.

Example: I hate her so much, she's such a whore.

Ich hasse sie so sehr, sie ist so eine Nutte.

3. Whore/Prostitute: *Hure*

Pronounced phonetically, it's easy to see how "hure" translates into the beloved insult "whore." In case you were reading through this guide, hoping for examples of the aforementioned English/German language similarities.

Explanation: Hure originated as a word to describe a prostitute in the medieval times. In the late 19th century it has been used to describe women who cheat on their spouses. Since the late 20th century it is also used to describe women who have a large number of sexual partners or wear permissive clothes. Hure is considered a harsh swear word and is mainly used by young people.

Example: That whore tried to steal my boyfriend.

Die Hure hat versucht mir meinen Freund zu klauen.

4. Pussy: *Pussy*

Nothing says "Nut up and face your fears" quite like calling someone a pussy (luckily it translates intact!). No matter what adventures you might find yourself embroiled in while you're in Germany, you'll want to be able to taunt your friends for being too scaredy-cat to go first. It might also come in handy if you somehow manage to get a German woman to come home with you and share your bed…but don't get your hopes up, Romeo.

Explanation: Pussy has the same meaning as the English swear word, however is also often used to describe an individual of physical weakness.

Example: My friend Hans is a nice guy but he's a pussy.

Mein Kumpel Hans ist ein netter Typ, aber er ist so eine Pussy.

5. Bimbo: *Tusse*

Calling someone a bimbo isn't usually a great thing, but there are positives to the kinds of women who might hear this word a lot. For example, bimbos make great arm candy. They're also usually a lot of fun (in fact, some of the most fun people out there). They know all about volumizing hair spray. And they look great rolling into your high school reunion on your arm…wait, we already said that one. Well, there are at least three positives should you find yourself a German bimbo while you're abroad.

Explanation: The origination of the word Tusse is unknown. It is argued that it originates from the hero Tusnelda in Heinrich von Kleists novel Hermannsschlacht, however the hero is strong and brave and therefore the exact opposite of a Tusse. It is guessed that it was created by students, who were sick of having to read the novel.

Tusse is a rather mild swear word and is not seen as vulgar. It is used by both young and old peoples, so you know it can't be that bad.

Example: Big hair and no brains, what a bimbo.

Tolle Haare und kein Gehirn, was eine Tusse.

6. Bimbo: *Schnäpfe*

Don't take it personally if you're visiting your old German granny and she leans over, pats your cheek affectionately and calls you a "Schnäpfe." Older generations always regard younger ones as rather foolish, and even if Granny does think you're an American-born ditz, she still loves you. Promise.

Explanation: Schnäpfe has originated as a word for a prostitute in the 19th century, however is now used in a milder form. Schnäpfe is a commonly used swear word in Germany. It is a very mild swear word and used by almost everyone.

Example: My husband's new secretary is a bimbo.

Die neue Sekretärin meines Mannes ist eine richtige Schnäpfe.

Insults for the Gentlemen

While women gain equal traction with men the world over, one place they will never have men beat is in something we can call the "jerk-off arena." This encompasses the male propensity for being jerks who think with their penises. As winners (if you could call them that) in this particular sport, men are particularly deserving of a whole host of insults and swear words, and the German language does not disappoint. Men can be thick-headed *and* thick-skinned, though, you're going to have to come out swinging if you want to knock someone out with your German shit-talking.

1. Son of a whore: *Hurensohn*

"Hurensohn" is another great example of the rather phonetic ways that English and German are related. While it makes a great insult when someone cuts you in line somewhere, it's equally satisfying as an exclamation of surprise or dismay, the way Americans like to say, "Son of a bitch!" when things don't quite go as planned.

Explanation: Hurensohn became a very popular swear word in the 1990's. Hure, the swear word for prostitute has been used as such for many years. Prostitution was seen as a dirty job in the past (and still is perceived as such by some people today), thus a prostitute and their children were seen as lower class citizens. Hurensohn is a rather harsh swear word and is mainly used by younger people. It is perceived as rather vulgar.

Example: That traffic warden just gave me a ticket. Son of a whore!

Der Polizist hat mir gerade ein Ticket verpasst. So ein Hurensohn!

2. Idiot: *Idiot*

"Idiot" occupies a special place in any vulgar person's vocabulary, as it is both casual and cutting. Said with the right insouciance, it conveys a definite air of superiority, combined with the promise of a more precise verbal beat-down should the object of the speaker's disdain not cease his mindless chatter. Lucky for English speakers, "idiot" translates intact; you'll just have to work on your accent.

Explanation: Idiot has the same meaning in German as it has in English.

Example: That guy is a complete idiot.

Dieser Typ ist ein totaler Idiot.

3. Idiot: *Dummkopf*

Even if the two aren't directly related, the first syllable of "Dummkopf" sounds a lot like "dumb," so if you want to sound fancier (to impress your German friends), try the former on for size.

Explanation: Dummkopf has been commonly used as a mild swear word since the 19th century. It has always had the same meaning; to describe a person of a lesser intelligence. Dummkopf is a mild swear word and commonly used in Germany by young and old people.

Example: That idiot thinks he knows what he's doing.

Der Dummkopf denkt, er weiss was er tut.

4. Spastic: *Spast*

It is always an interesting exercise to speculate where words got their beginnings, as in the case of "Spast" and its relation to "spastic." Since we're not worried about being too politically correct in this guide (as we assume you, dear student of the German language, must not be — why else would you be reading this?), you can just go ahead and use this word on anyone you think is acting like a random fool.

Explanation: "Spastiker" comes from the greek word *spasmos* and describes a physical handicap caused by a malfunction of the nervous system. The word has been used in the past to describe someone with this disease and originated as a popular swear word in the 1990s. Spast is seen as a harsh swear word and mainly used by younger people.

Example: Did you see Jurgen try and skateboard? What a Spastic.

Hast du gesehen wie Jürgen versucht hat Skateboard zu fahren? So ein Spast.

5. Retard: *Zabel*

Never forget: in the German language, you have options when you want to call someone out for acting like they have a handicap. "Zabel" and "Spast" are obviously and closely related, but the former denigrates people with mental problems, the latter, people with physical ailments.

Explanation: Zabel originates from a movie about a mongoloid boy named Walter Zabbel. The movie came out in the 1970s, however the swear word only started becoming very popular in the 1980s. Zabel is a very common swear word among young people. It is seen as a very politically incorrect swear word and therefore not very often used by older people.

Example: That guy looks like a retard.

Der Typ sieht aus wie ein Zabel.

6. Wanker: *Wichser*

Those sassy Brits use "wanker" quite a bit, and while it's not so common in the States, you can still hear people reference the word now and then ("I was wanking off last night…" your friend's horrific story might begin). The Germans certainly aren't going to miss an opportunity to make fun of someone by referring to them by a masturbatory term.

Explanation: *Wichsen* has become popular as a word for masturbation in the late 20th century. *Wichsen* originally meant polishing or cleaning something. Wichser is a rather harsh swear word, however is commonly used. It is mainly used by the younger population and is considered a very vulgar swear word.

Example: If I see that wanker again I'm going to tell him just what I think of him.

Wenn ich diesen Wichser nochmal sehe, werde ich ihm erzählen, was ich über ihn denke.

7. Asshole: *Arschloch*

"Asshole" is like the chocolate of swear words. It goes with anything! And while there is such a thing as too much of a good thing, we believe that there are near-infinite flavor combinations that will keep your taste buds from tiring of the word "asshole," and its German counterpart, for a very, very long time.

Explanation: Arschloch is a harsh word to describe the anus. It has been used as such and as a swear word since the 19th century. Arschloch is considered a rather mild swear word and is therefore used by almost everyone. It is one of the most commonly used swear words in Germany.

Example: Hey asshole, don't even think of trying to steal my parking space.

Hey, du Arschloch, denk gar nicht daran meinen Parkplatz zu klauen.

Equal-opportunity Insults,
Slang Terms and Exclamations

While you are visiting Germany you might stub your toe. Or get cut off in traffic. Or (heaven forbid) get robbed. In those instances you might not be able to see who instigated your latest adventure in woe, so you will need to yell something in your anger that addresses everyone — or no one (except yourself, anyway). In those cases, we bring you these equal-opportunity insults and other curse words that might not fix your problem, but could make you feel better about it, even for just a second.

1. Shut up: Halt's Maul

Literally "hold your mouth," *Halt's Maul* is perfect for situations where you need to make the running commentary from that one non-stop chit-chatty friend end abruptly (or else lose your mind). It is direct and to-the-point without being overly insensitive, which is a good tone to take when you're addressing someone you would actually like to hang out with again.

Explanation: The word was originally used by farmers as a form of degradation as Maul refers to the mouth of an animal. The expression is very commonly used in Germany by almost everyone as it is a rather mild swear word. It can be used in a joking manner as well.

Example: Shut up or I will slap you!

Halt den Mund, oder ich verpass dir eine!

2. Shut up: *Halt die Klappe*

"Hold the flap"? Well I never! While your mouth might not be the "flappiest" part on your body (we'll reserve judgment), it is certainly the part with which most people lead, no matter what continent they're on. Some people just cannot keep their mouths shut and always have to offer an opinion (that no one asked for), advice (totally unsolicited) or a random observation (awesome, thanks!). Now you know how to shut down the German mouth-runners, as well as American ones.

Explanation: The expression comes from the medieval times. Monks went to the church daily to pray and had to sit on wooden folding chairs, which they had to hold and release slowly so that the chairs would not snap back and make loud noises. If someone forgot to do so he was scolded with *Halt die Klappe*. *Halt die Klappe* is a mild swear word. It is commonly used by children and adults.

Example: Shut up, I'm not listening to you anymore.

Halt die Klappe, ich höre dir nicht mehr zu.

3. Fuck you: *Fick dich*

Surprised that it has taken this long to get to the King of All Curse Words? Good things come to those who wait. "Fuck" is an immensely satisfying and versatile expression, but "fuck you" gets right to the point — the point being, whoever you are addressing is garbage, and at least right at this very moment, you hate them. Hopefully your visit to Germany is a pleasant one, and you never have any problems with anyone, but "Fick dich" is like sunblock: you should pack it, because it never hurts to be prepared.

Explanation: Ficken means having sex with someone and originated as a popular swear word in the 1980s. In the past ficken meant rubbing or moving something fast. This is a rather harsh swear word and mostly used by younger people. It is mostly used in an angry manner; on very few occasions it is used in a joking manner between young people.

Example: Fuck you, you don't know anything!

Fick dich, du hast doch keine Ahnung!

4. Shit: *Scheisse*

"Shit" is almost as good as "fuck" when it comes to the variety of situations where it can be used, and it's slightly less obscene, which may be good to keep in mind if you're anywhere near old people, coworkers, teachers or some combination of the three. In America we use it as an exclamation of dismay, as well as a coarse word for excrement, and it's actually considered a cause for greater censorship here in the States than in Germany (where it's more like saying "crap").

Explanation: Scheisse is a vulgar word for faeces and has been used since the 20th century in order to describe negative things or situations. Scheisse is a rather mild swear word and used by almost everyone, young and old. It can refer to people, situations and things.

Example: My football team is total shit this year.

Mein Fußballverein ist total scheiße dieses Jahr.

5. Poop: *Kacke*

You ever wonder why people refer to poo as "kacka" or similar? Here is your answer. While we get beautiful loan words from France and Italy, we get "Kacke" from Germany, but that's okay. They rained kacka down on the world during the first half of the 20th century, so this particular linguistic legacy is more than appropriate. Plus, speaking of appropriate, you could probably say this to your elderly aunt without getting smacked.

Explanation: Kacke originated in the 16th century as a word for pooping and has been used as a swear word since the 20th century. Kacke is the milder version of scheisse (shit) and commonly used by young and old.

Example: My homework is poop.

Meine Hausaufgaben sind kacke.

6. Damn: *Mist*

"Damn" almost isn't a swear word at this point in time, though if you hear someone's five-year-old say it at an inappropriate moment, it's invariably hilarious. You probably won't get into much trouble in Germany by saying "mist" while you're out and about, unless anyone super conservative is in earshot. Since you don't want to alienate any of the locals while you're visiting, put "mist" on your must list — as in, "I must watch my mouth, even if I bite my tongue and it hurts a lot!"

Explanation: Mist has been used since the 10th century as a word for manure and has become a popular swear word in the 19th century. Mist is a milder version of scheisse (shit) and very commonly used in Germany by everyone. It is not seen as a vulgar swear word.

Example: Damn, my exam is tomorrow. I thought it was next week.

Mist, meine Klausur ist morgen. Ich dachte die wäre erst nächste Woche.

7. Damn: *Verdammt*

"Verdammt" looks rather more recognizable than "mist" in relation to the word "damn," so perhaps you'll remember this one better. It is applied in a different way, though; think of it as "I'll be damned!" — an expression we use a lot in America, and which you might use a lot more in Germany, especially if you tour any of their historic sites, like their castles. Surely the impressed look on your face will translate well, too.

Explanation: "Verdammt" in the past was used as a word to describe the action of being condemned to go to hell. It is now commonly used as an expression to express happy feelings, surprised feelings, as well as anger. "Verdammt" is a rather mild swear word and is not considered a very vulgar word. It is therefore commonly used by young, as well as old German people.

Example: Damn, I just got ketchup on my nice clean shirt.

Verdammt, ich hab gerade Ketchup auf mein schönes, sauberes Shirt geschüttet.

8. This is retarded: *Das ist behindert*

If your tour guide in a German museum won't let you touch any of the incredible-looking weapons on display, you have two choices: listen to him or her and keep your hands to yourself; or, you can say "Das ist behindert," and then keep your hands to yourself. At least with the latter option you conveyed a sense of the rampant injustice to which you were subjected and got to show off your sass mouth in German.

Explanation: Behindert means handicapped and has been used in the past and is still used to describe physical and mental handicaps. It originated as a popular swear word in the 1980s. As this swear word mocks people with a physical or mental handicap it is seen as very politically incorrect and mainly used by younger people.

Example: I have so much work to do but haven't been given any proper instructions. This is retarded.

Ich habe so viel Arbeit zu tun, aber mir wurden keine richtigen Anweisungen gegeben. Das ist doch behindert.

9. Fuck off: *Verpiss dich*

The "piss" in "Verpiss" is no coincidence, and this vulgar little gem is like saying "Piss off" or "Piss the fuck off" in English. While "piss" and "fuck" are both great on their own, it's easy to see the merit in combining the two — with a bit of a German growl, very menacing — to really get some annoying loser to leave you alone while you try and hit on someone cute at a bar.

Explanation: *Verpiss dich* originated during the second world war. *Pissen* means to piss. Going for a piss had been the only possibility for soldiers to leave the front for a minute. It has been used as a popular swear word since the 1980s. Verpiss dich is seen as a vulgar swear word and mainly used by younger people.

Example: Fuck off or you are going to get hurt!

Verpiss dich, oder ich tu dir weh!

10. This sucks: *Das ist beschissen*

Flight get delayed? Sudden freak rainstorm while you're out in the German countryside? Grumpy German aunt insists you join her and her friends for a card game? Respond — perhaps none too loudly with the last scenario — with a passionate "*Das ist beschissen*!" It might not change your situation, but it could make you feel better to get the sentiment off your chest.

Explanation: Beschissen is the adverb of scheisse. Scheisse is a vulgar word for faeces and has been used since the 20th century in order to describe negative things or situations. Das ist beschissen is a swear word of medium harshness. It is commonly used by old and young, however is seen as a vulgar expression. The literal meaning is "this is covered in shit."

Example: What do you mean I can't go out tonight? This sucks!

Was meinst du damit, ich kann heute Abend nicht weggehen? Das ist beschissen!

11. Go away: *Hau ab*

There are definitely some things you can't say to a coworker or fellow student in Germany, because they'll report you for being crude. However, "Hau ab" is relatively harmless and shouldn't get you into any trouble. After all, how else are you supposed to tell someone leave you alone? *Verpiss dich* could get you fired or suspended! *Hau ab* will probably get you a glare or a sigh at worst.

Explanation: The verb abhauen literally means fleeing. *Hau ab* has been used as a swear word and expression of anger since the the 18th century. *Hau ab* is a rather mild swear word, commonly used by everyone in Germany. It can be used as an angry expression to tell people to go away or as a statement to express surprise ("Get outta here!")

Example: Go away, you are really annoying me!

Hau ab, du nervst mich wirklich!

Printed in Great Britain
by Amazon